The Political Structure
of the Federal
Health Planning Program

The Political Structure
of the Federal
Health Planning Program

A Staff Paper by Lawrence D. Brown

THE BROOKINGS INSTITUTION
Washington, D.C.

Copyright © 1982 by
THE BROOKINGS INSTITUTION
1775 Massachusetts Avenue, N.W., Washington, D.C. 20036

Reproduced, after minor editorial revisions, from *Health Planning in the United States: Selected Policy Issues,* Volume 2, 1981, by permission of the National Academy of Sciences, Washington, D.C. No claim of copyright is entered for those portions of this paper taken verbatim from that source.

Library of Congress Catalog Card Number 81-70468
ISBN 0-8157-1159-X

1 2 3 4 5 6 7 8 9

THE BROOKINGS INSTITUTION is an independent organization devoted to nonpartisan research, education, and publication in economics, government, foreign policy, and the social sciences generally. Its principal purposes are to aid in the development of sound public policies and to promote public understanding of issues of national importance.

The Institution was founded on December 8, 1927, to merge the activities of the Institute for Government Research, founded in 1916, the Institute of Economics, founded in 1922, and the Robert Brookings Graduate School of Economics and Government, founded in 1924.

The Board of Trustees is responsible for the general administration of the Institution, while the immediate direction of the policies, program, and staff is vested in the President, assisted by an advisory committee of the officers and staff. The by-laws of the Institution state: "It is the function of the Trustees to make possible the conduct of scientific research, and publication, under the most favorable conditions, and to safeguard the independence of the research staff in the pursuit of their studies and in the publication of the results of such studies. It is not a part of their function to determine, control, or influence the conduct of particular investigations or the conclusions reached."

The President bears final responsibility for the decision to publish a manuscript as a Brookings book. In reaching his judgment on the competence, accuracy, and objectivity of each study, the President is advised by the director of the appropriate research program and weighs the views of a panel of expert outside readers who report to him in confidence on the quality of the work. Publication of a work signifies that it is deemed a competent treatment worthy of public consideration but does not imply endorsement of conclusions or recommendations.

The Institution maintains its position of neutrality on issues of public policy in order to safeguard the intellectual freedom of the staff. Hence interpretations or conclusions in Brookings publications should be understood to be solely those of the authors and should not be attributed to the Institution, to its trustees, officers, or other staff members, or to the organizations that support its research.

Foreword

The Health Planning and Resources Development Act of 1974 created a national network of new health systems agencies to devise and implement broad-ranging health plans that would achieve a better match between local needs and resources. Supervised by both state agencies and the federal government, these agencies were expected to adequately reflect their communities: the governing boards were to have a consumer majority, and local providers, racial groups, and other relevant interests were to be well represented. The planning program, in short, set out to do rational planning using the methods of grass roots democracy.

Almost from the beginning, controversy has characterized the complex health planning program and its ambitious goals. Critics have charged that the health systems agencies are either "provider dominated" or too "interest inclusive" to be cohesive; that they are either too concerned about cost containment, not concerned enough, or simply unfocused; and that they are either lacking in sanctions or have used their powers to harass providers and interfere with competitive processes. Some believe the agencies have had insufficient time and money to make a showing; others charge that they have wasted both time and money. In 1981, after the Reagan administration sought to eliminate all federal funds for the planning program, some congressmen attempted to keep the program alive, but it is clear that federally sponsored health planning faces an uncertain future.

In this paper, Lawrence D. Brown, a research associate in the Brookings Governmental Studies program, discusses the major strengths and weaknesses of health planning in the United States. By examining the internal organizational politics of the planning agency and its political position among other organizations at all three levels of the federal system, Brown tries to assess what local health planning bodies can and cannot be expected to accomplish.

This essay appeared in substantially its present form as "Some Structural Issues in the Health Planning Program," originally published in Institute of Medicine, *Health Planning in the United States: Selected Policy Issues,* vol. 2 (Washington, D.C.: National Academy Press, January 1981). The research was supported by a grant to Brookings from the National Center for Health Services Research, Office of the Assistant Secretary for Health.

The author is grateful to Christa Altenstetter, Robert Derzon, Judith Feder, William Glaser, Adela J. Gondek, Charyl Kiger, Bonnie Lefkowitz, Louise Russell, and Jessica Townsend for their valuable comments on the manuscript. He also thanks former colleagues at the Institut für Medizinische Informatik und Systemforschung in Munich for explaining the rudiments of the West German health care system.

The views expressed here are those of the author and should not be ascribed to the persons and organizations whose assistance is acknowledged above or to the trustees, officers, or other staff members of the Brookings Institution.

BRUCE K. MACLAURY
President

Washington, D.C.
December 1981

The Political Structure
of the Federal
Health Planning Program

"We designed it backwards."—*Federal Official*

That planning is inseparable from politics is a truism. The corollary—that planning is therefore also inseparable from political structure—is less familiar.[1] Political "structures"—the explicit distribution of roles and powers among official participants in a public program and the informal distribution that both official and unofficial participants invent to supplement these explicit arrangements—do much to define the rules of the policy game and the balance of power among interests.

A new federal program raises three central structural questions: first, how the program will be organized internally (organizational questions); second, how it will fit with existing programs in its immediate (usually state or local) environment (environmental questions); and third, what requirements, regulations, and informal understandings will bind it to its federal creators and administrators (federal questions). These questions are especially important when the federal government tries to meet its objectives by creating and working through a new organization—for example, the Health Systems Agency (HSA) network with which this paper deals. An organization-building effort of this kind goes beyond altering organizational and intergovernmental arrangements at the margin by means of new requirements and incentives attached to grants-in-aid. Instead, it injects a

1. As Christa Altenstetter points out: "During the past 25 years or so, comparative studies on political systems . . . have focused attention on politics and *processes*, assuming that *structure* had little or no influence in shaping these processes. . . ." *Health Policy-Making and Administration in West Germany and the United States* (Beverly Hills: Sage Publications, 1974), p. 8 (emphasis in original).

1

new organizational presence, a new structure, into the existing set of programs. Building a new organization is more complicated than deciding what conditions to attach to grants-in-aid. Fitting a new organization into the universe of state and local organizations is more complex than trying to alter the behavior of some member of that universe in delimited respects. Trying to decide how the trade-off between federal control and local autonomy affects the capacities of a new organization is more difficult than attempting to assert "the influence of federal grants" incrementally over time in established programs.[2]

These structural questions are highly pertinent in the health planning field, where organization-building has been central to the federal government's strategy.[3] In 1974, convinced that the nation needed a network of area- and state-based health planning bodies but that the comprehensive health planning (CHP) agencies created in 1966 had proved to be too weak, the federal government set out to strengthen the CHP model. The HSAs were the health planning bodies established by the Health Planning and Resources Development Act of 1974 (Public Law 93-641). In each state one HSA or more would assume responsibility for drawing up long-term "health systems plans" (HSPs) and "annual implementation plans" (AIPs) that considered the needs of their jurisdictions and whether present and projected resources and resource development patterns were adequate. The agency would be run by a governing board whose structure was set forth in considerable detail. It was to be composed of representatives of consumers, providers, and local organizations and of special income, racial, linguistic, and other groups. Consumers were required to constitute a majority of the board. As of November 1979 there were 202 HSAs, 16 of which crossed state lines and 12 of which covered an entire state.[4]

The law also prescribed new intergovernmental arrangements. To assure coordination and planning on the proper scale, it required that the work of the HSAs within each state be coordinated by a single State Health Planning and Development Agency (SHPDA), which would synthesize HSA plans into a statewide plan subject in turn to the approval of a State-

2. The quoted phrase is from Martha Derthick, *The Influence of Federal Grants* (Harvard University Press, 1970).

3. The organization-building strategy has also been prominent in federal health efforts other than planning. Neighborhood health centers, health maintenance organizations, and professional standards review organizations are the leading additional examples.

4. U.S. Department of Health, Education, and Welfare, Health Resources Administration, "Directory: Health Systems Agencies, State Health Planning and Development Agencies, Statewide Health Coordinating Councils," November 1, 1979.

wide Health Coordinating Council (SHCC), a majority of whose members would come from HSAs within the state. The plans would be considered by federal grant-giving agencies in the review of applications for funds (so-called proposed use of federal funds, or PUFF, reviews) and by the state in reviewing the application of each health care institution for its "certificates of need."[5] These state and local bodies are themselves subject to regulations and guidelines issued by the Department of Health and Human Services (formerly the Department of Health, Education, and Welfare), which is advised by a National Council on Health Planning and Resources Development.

Thus the federal government has chosen to strengthen health planning in the United States by establishing new local, state, and federal organizations and by conferring on them significant planning responsibilities and regulatory powers. These powers, stronger than review and comment but weaker than review and sign-off, are rather modest regulatory weapons. Yet the powers, and still more the presence, of the HSAs, SHPDAs, and SHCCs are of considerable political importance. The official expression of a federally created "voice of the people" on health planning questions can legitimate or impugn professional, institutional, and grass roots initiatives and can thereby help shape the nature of health care debates and perhaps even tip the balance of power in state and local health politics decisively to one side or the other.

This paper, which summarizes impressions drawn from the author's research in progress on the implementation of health planning and regulatory efforts in the states of Maryland, Washington, Michigan, and New York, addresses the question whether the structural arrangements adopted by the federal government for health planning are adequate to the ambitious goals set for the planning process. When one evaluates the structure of such a program, the level of detail is not a sure indicator of the level of sophistication. Program designers may address structural questions in minute detail and still miss the most important ones. Details may stem from a realistic and dispassionate understanding of institutional patterns "out there," or they may reflect the designers' ideologies, certain intuitively or widely held prejudices about "how things work," or the need to smooth

5. A certificate of need is a document required by state law attesting that a public (state) agency has studied a capital expenditure planned by a hospital or other health care institution and has judged it to be needed by the community and otherwise in the public interest. About half the states had enacted such laws by 1974, when the planning law required that all states enact them by 1980.

rough legislative edges to win the support or assuage the opposition of important groups.

As Raab has demonstrated, the structure of the planning system strongly reflected the values and world view of its designers, especially of the congressional staffs who developed the legislation in detail.[6] The designers took a dim view of the contribution of state and local politicians and administrators to health planning: the parochialism of the politicians and administrators, their susceptibility to interest-group influence, and their general inefficiencies, it was thought, made it highly desirable to limit their planning roles.[7] Thus in most cases the HSAs were not to be public agencies but private, nonprofit ones. But if the designers disdained conventional politics, they valued pluralism highly. They recognized that providers, consumers, and other community interests must be involved in plan development and viewed the HSA as a suitable forum for working out their differences precisely *because* it was a new and self-contained organization, at arm's length from the pols and civil servants. Even so the "partisan mutual adjustment" of interest group interaction was not what the designers had in mind:[8] the planning process was to be rigorous, technocratic, and rational.[9] Presumably these qualities were thought to follow from the emphasis the designers placed on checks and balances, on fashioning a structure that would withstand the dominance of politician, bureaucrat, and professional alike—indeed of any single special interest. Agencies endowed with the countervailing power of a consumer majority and an admixture of various community factions would arrive at a reasonable and efficient understanding of the community's true interest and then embody it in plans.

There is room for disagreement about whether this blend of antipolitical animus, pluralism, technocracy, and countervailing power was a coup of

6. George Gregory Raab, "Health Planning and American Federalism" (Ph.D. dissertation, University of Virginia, 1980).

7. As it turned out, however, the planning law and regulations granted very considerable powers to the states. See ibid. and Drew Altman, "The Politics of Health Care Regulation: The Case of the National Health Planning and Resources Development Act," *Journal of Health Politics, Policy, and Law*, vol. 2 (Winter 1978), pp. 560–80, especially pp. 565–72.

8. The term "partisan mutual adjustment" is from Charles Lindblom, *The Intelligence of Democracy* (Free Press, 1965).

9. "A pervasive belief underlying the legislation is that planning is a mechanistic enterprise, a matter of developing and applying technical expertise. The central process of mechanistic planning is the development of objective, numerical standards to rationalize the health facilities system and to determine scientifically the correct health care investments to be made." Randall Bovbjerg, "Problems and Prospects for Health Planning: The Importance of Incentives, Standards, and Procedures in Certificate of Need," *Utah Law Review*, vol. 1978, no. 1 (1978), p. 93.

theoretical ingenuity or a fatuously implausible construct. It is beyond doubt, however, that the cohesion of this precarious assemblage of values and processes depends heavily on the structure of the HSA and its related institutions. If for some reason the HSA organizations fail to work as intended, the premises of the program cannot be maintained and the expected conclusions do not follow. It is useful, therefore, to turn to the three structural questions mentioned at the start of this paper—organizational, environmental, and federal—and to examine the realism of the designers' work.

The HSA as an Organization

An examination of the organizational structure of an HSA usually, and properly, begins with an analysis of the HSA board. In 1977, for example, Bruce Vladeck persuasively argued that the HSA strategy and structure are in many ways at odds. Assembling around a table representatives of a wide range of local interests is unlikely to produce the dispassionate and rational planning modeled in the texts. Instead, it creates a highly politicized body in which the surest road to consensus is the splitting of particularistic and parochial differences by means of bargaining, logrolling, and pork-barreling.[10]

The HSAs' behavior cannot be entirely predicted from the composition of their governing boards, however, for these boards are but the tip of an organizational iceberg. The boards consist of part-time volunteers meeting intermittently to consider proposals developed in other settings. These other settings, the work units of the organization, deserve attention in their own right. First, however, it is necessary to consider the nature of an HSA's work.

The HSA's mandated mission is broad, complex, and ambiguous. According to one account, "The agency's primary responsibility is the provision of effective health planning for its area and the promotion of the development (within the area) of health services, manpower, and facilities which meet identified needs, reduce documented inefficiencies and imple-

10. Bruce C. Vladeck, "Interest-Group Representation and the HSAs: Health Planning and Political Theory," *American Journal of Public Health*, vol. 32 (January 1977), pp. 238–54; and Aaron Wildavsky, "Can Health Be Planned?" 1976 Michael M. Davis Lecture, Center for Health Administrative Studies, Graduate School of Business, University of Chicago.

ment the health plans of the agency."[11] This definition emphasizes planning and promotion. Yet the same acccount implies that the heart of the HSAs' mission may be mainly research. For example: "The Plans must . . . describe and characterize the status of the entire health system, noting the effects that changes in one part of the system may have on other parts. . . ." They must emphasize "a systemwide approach with specified, quantified goals, and the addition of information on costs and financing (and the effects of proposed goals on cost containment goals). . . ." Moreover, "the agency must consider the array of influences on health. In developing their plans . . . agencies are expected to identify all relevant health factors and problems . . . and where possible isolate those conditions which can be addressed by the delivery system. . . ."[12]

In practice, however, it appears that a fourth mission may be most important: cost containment by means of regulating capital investment. A recent study of health planning in New England found that most of the agencies studied "accept regulation as their first priority."[13] And according to Basil Mott, "cost containment is the driving force behind P.L. 93-641."[14]

There appear, then, to be at least four distinct components to the HSA mission: research, planning, regulation, and advocacy (promotion). Unfortunately, organizational arrangements suitable for one of these tasks may not be suitable for others. For example, the very systematic and ambitious research envisioned will require the skills of highly trained academic experts and will take years. Planning presupposes an adequate research base to support the plans but requires a rather different mix of skills, not the ability to do research but rather the capacity to understand it and to apply it intelligently and flexibly to the specifics of a local situation. Regulation calls for a high degree of legal and political skill, for it entails the application of a plan to institutions and the defense of those applications against the laments (and suits) of aggrieved interests. Advocacy, finally, requires a talent for reducing complex matters to readily understandable terms, the rhetorical power to stir the blood, and the organizational ability to mobilize

11. Harry P. Cain II and Helen B. Darling, "Health Planning in the United States: Where We Stand Today," *Health Policy and Education*, vol. 1 (Spring 1979), p. 10.

12. Ibid., pp. 15–16.

13. The Codman Research Group, Inc., *Health Planning and Regulation: The New England Experience, Final Report*, vol. 1, pt. 1 (September 30, 1979), p. 70. (Hereinafter, Codman Report.)

14. Basil J. F. Mott, "The New Health Planning System," in Arthur Levin, ed., *Health Services: The Local Perspective*, Proceedings of the Academy of Political Science, vol. 32, no. 3 (1977), p. 241.

some community interests for and against others. It is difficult to picture one agency performing well all four tasks simultaneously.

Given the breadth, diversity, and complexity of the HSA missions, it is not surprising that participants sometimes express uncertainty about the nature of their enterprise. As the executive director of an HSA in Washington State said in an interview: "A basic underlying problem is, it's sort of like building a ship. It's a big enterprise. You have to put all the parts together. But it's not been decided what kind of ship it's going to be, or even if it's going to be a ship, or what it's evolving toward." Some even appear to doubt whether the HSAs are principally health agencies at all. Thus Checkoway cites one director who describes the HSA as a "social planning agency focusing on health" and another who views it as "an agency for social change."[15]

A rationally designed program presumably would begin by deciding the "outputs" it wishes to achieve, would then prescribe "processes" (activities) that support those ends, and would finally define the "inputs" (personnel and other resources) needed to sustain those processes. The intended outputs of the planning process may be interpreted to be anything from cost containment to social change, with many ambiguous possibilities in between. The prescribed processes encompass research, planning, regulation, and advocacy. And it is questionable that the participatory, corporative structure of the HSAs is well suited to support any, let alone all, of these processes.

Because each of the various ends and activities has influential proponents, HSAs must attempt in practice to honor all of them. In essence, the HSA mission is to assemble a representative and committed subset of community volunteers and then bring these members together to canvass rigorously and scientifically virtually the entire range of health needs and resources in the community, compare (in some sense) needs with resources, devise a long-range plan that rationally relates needs to resources, and then rework the long-term plan into a short-term plan of sufficient clarity and specificity that it may serve as a defensible basis for making detailed decisions about resources and services in the area. It need hardly be said that these are not easy tasks. No one knows how to make these judgments. Although various planning methodologies may be culled from the literature, none is self-evidently correct, and partisans dispute hotly about the

15. Barry Checkoway, "Consumerism in Health Planning Agencies," in Institute of Medicine, *Health Planning in the United States: Selected Policy Issues*, vol. 2: *Papers* (Washington, D.C.: National Academy Press, January 1981), p. 160.

merits of different approaches.[16] The problem is aggravated by the HSA structure, which transforms the agency's environment into organizational participants. HSA board members meet collectively only on occasion, and many may be only casually interested in the matter at hand. But that matter may be of intense and immediate concern to a subset of board members or to well-connected executives of local health care organizations. Therefore, if the HSA is to go beyond the formulation of bland and nonspecific plans, it must be prepared to fight within its own ranks and in the community for the stand it takes.

The central organizational problem of the HSAs is how to make their herculean tasks—nearly impossible to achieve[17]—more manageable. Their response is the age-old expedient of division of labor; that is, they divide their members and staff into subgroups and ask them to specialize in portions of the tasks at hand. Division of labor in HSAs takes three main forms: committees, staff, and subarea councils. The heart of HSA decision-making is to be found in these three subunits. But these subunits, vital as they are to the organization's workings, also act as centrifugal forces, pulling control away from the center (the executive director and the board) and fragmenting the agency's identity and unity of viewpoint. HSA management is therefore a constant and sometimes hopeless struggle to reconcile the virtues of comprehensive planning with the virtues of decentralized work groups.

Committees

Like other organizations facing complex tasks, the HSA's first and basic response to complexity is to break it up and farm it out. Thus an HSA usually divides its board members into a half-dozen or more subject-matter committees, each composed of perhaps a dozen or so members, roughly half consumer and half provider.[18] Committees tend to be of four general types: (1) administration—personnel, budget, and so on (no further account will be taken of it here); (2) need assessment—primary care, mental

16. A good example is the recurring argument over the merits of process versus outcome measures in health planning. See the discussion in George W. Downs, "Monitoring the Health Planning System: Data, Measurement and Inference Problems," in ibid., pp. 81–103.

17. Mott, "The New Health Planning System," p. 241.

18. In amendments to the original law, however, "A consumer majority is required for all subcommittees or advisory bodies appointed by an HSA governing board or executive committee." U.S. Department of Health, Education, and Welfare, Health Resources Administration, "Health Planning Amendments of 1979: A Summary," n.d., p. 5.

health, prevention, and the like, committees that concentrate on documenting and advancing neglected needs and services; (3) regulatory—especially facilities and grant review; and (4) plan development—drawing up the long- and short-term plans on which HSA decisions are expected to rest, or at any rate with which they are supposed to be consistent. The committees institutionalize a split personality in the agency. Need assessment committees make it their business to act as spokesmen for more and new services. Regulatory committees are asked to make constraining decisions that require trimming fat and arguing for "less." There is no logical reason why the two tasks must conflict, why denying new acute care beds to a hospital must complicate assessment of the need for a new outpatient clinic. In many cases, complications do arise, however. One reason is that meeting needs may require new grant funds or new facilities. Another is that hospitals themselves may suggest such compromises as expansion of outpatient services in exchange for a favorable HSA recommendation on a bed expansion, modernization project, or new piece of equipment. In these cases, relations between the need assessment and regulatory committees can become confused or conflictual, and the plan development committees, expected to produce a document that both saves money and does justice to the community's real (including its unmet) needs, may get caught in the cross fire.

Aggregating committee positions into a united agency stand is further complicated by the need for plan development committees to assume a holistic, system-wide perspective, while the need assessment and regulatory committees adopt what might be termed an "institutional" orientation. Their decisions turn on such questions as whether institution X is doing all it could for, say, the cause of health education, whether it has demonstrated that the community needs its proposed construction or modernization project, and so forth.

Staff

Because their members are part-time volunteers and their tasks are very broad and complex, HSAs depend heavily on full-time staff. Yet staff recruitment is often more difficult than recruiting members of the board. HSAs are new bodies, with uncertain futures and sometimes fairly remote locations; they therefore offer uncertain career prospects and relatively low salaries. None of this necessarily bothers board members, who have volunteered their interest in health planning, call their communities their home, participate "on the side," and do not get paid. All of it, however, may trouble staffers who wish to advance their careers, may be compelled to relocate families, will work for the HSA full time, and must make a decent living. For these reasons, an HSA staff position is likely to be attractive mainly to young men and women with master's degrees in health planning or administration (or related fields), who often are hesitating between a personal or ideological commitment to planning and public service on the one hand, and the practical advantages of a university doctoral program, a job in the private sector, or a civil service career on the other hand. Staff members, then, are plan-oriented; they are offered an HSA job because they are thought to command the how-to-do-it methodological skills of which planning is thought to consist, and they accept the offer because they are eager to practice their planning skills in the public interest, at least for a time.[19]

Staffs are indispensable, but integrating a corps of planning experts into a multifactional, lay-dominated HSA poses problems. First, suitable staff members are difficult to recruit and retain. For several reasons—clashes with the agency's director, isolated location of the agency, low salaries, and heavy work loads, for example[20]—high staff turnover has been a problem for many HSAs. Turnover means not only the loss of manpower but also in many cases the loss of the one person, or the few, who truly understood (or claimed to understand) the arcane assumptions and quantitative methods that support the plan. When the staffer who patiently and at length managed to persuade the members of the facilities review committee and then the HSA board as a whole that the Walsh-Bicknell approach is the one true method of evaluating certificate of need (CON) applications departs and is replaced by a colleague with severe reservations about Walsh-Bicknell but

19. Many staff members soon turn to practicing these skills in the private sector. As the Codman Report (p. 40) observed: "The turnover is high on HSA staffs and in state agencies with the forwarding addresses often being state hospital associations, PSROs [professional standards review organizations] or major hospitals. The first head of certificate of need review in Massachusetts left to join a Boston teaching hospital. Her successor recently quit also, taking a post at a major suburban community hospital. Their colleague responsible for the preparation of planning standards is now with the hospital association in an adjoining state. Several HSA staff members also now work for hospital councils or local providers. No one can say judgments of regulators are compromised by the prospects of future employment with the industry; no one can say they are not either."

20. The list is taken from Lorabeth Lawson, "Evaluation of the Performance of HSA's in Region X and Implications for Future Technical Assistance Efforts: Summary Findings," Discussion Paper 13 (Center for Health Services Research, Department of Health Services, University of Washington, April 1979), p. 4.

full confidence in a rival method, the ensuing "reorienting and training and a new approach to the planning process" may leave consumers and providers alike glassy-eyed and disgusted.[21]

Even if staff tenure is long, however, the danger remains that the laymen will feel taken in or otherwise ill served by the staff. Staffs tend to make an odd mix with local consumers and medical professionals on the board and in committees, most of whom know a lot about their communities and institutions and little about the formalities of planning. Whereas board and committee members are apt to emphasize the particular needs, roles, and failings of particular institutions, staffs are inclined to concentrate on the proper role of one institution in the context of others, that is, in the overall plan. Volunteers may consider the staff to be unduly rigid and obsessed with the integrity of the plan and may fear that they are being pushed or backed by staff into positions they do not really want to endorse. In the words of the Consumer Coalition for Health:

> Many participants in the planning process, consumer and provider alike, complain about staff control of information, deadlines, etc. Staff *rarely* are willing to present controversial alternatives to planning decisions, i.e., analyses of the actual *effectiveness* of medical technology being purchased, expanded options as to how money might best be used, etc. . . . Consumers rarely become interested in health planning *per se*. They become interested because of specific issues: access, barriers, quality, costs. HSA staff rarely help consumers learn how to use the HSA's powers to solve these problems. Instead, the consumers are led a merry chase through HSPs, AIPs, square footage formulae, and debt ratios, etc. Small wonder that there are so many drop-outs.[22]

The staff skills required in an HSA are more than merely methodological. Politically sophisticated staff members, of whom there are many, work closely with consumer members of the HSA to resist "provider dominance" and help pull the agency together in defense of stands unpopular in the community. Not all staff members are politically adept, however, and even those who are may find managing the many conflicts that arise in the HSA's complex intraorganizational and interorganizational milieu—conflicts within and between committees, within and between consumer and provider factions, and within and between the HSA as a whole and the community, for example—to be an exhausting and perhaps impossible job.

21. Ibid.
22. Consumer Coalition for Health, "Written Submission to the Institute of Medicine Panel on Consumer Participation in Health Planning," April 9, 1980, p. 405 (emphasis in the original).

Subarea Councils

Many of the HSAs are built on the geographical, organizational, and personal foundations of the older CHP agencies, and many—by one count 105 of the 205 HSA areas[23]—retain the subarea councils to which CHP was often delegated. Local area-oriented activists who have become accustomed to speaking for the needs of their communities may be reluctant to blend their voices with that of a new regional HSA presence, that is, a central office executive director, board, and staff. Because subarea councils are often the source of nominations for positions on the HSA board, the subareas may be the board members' principal constituencies, and this in turn may make the board members solicitous of subarea autonomy.

One West Coast HSA, for example, tried to resolve these tensions by describing itself as a federation. Soon, impressed by experience and by federal complaints that a loose assemblage of warmed-over subarea documents was not "planning," it resolved to avoid the term "federation" and to build a strong central capacity to assert a system-wide perspective. (Its success to date has been very limited.) These tensions can be severe when subarea councils and HSA facilities review committees clash over who is to be the agency's true spokesman for local certificate of need reviews. They are most severe when an expansion-minded rural, underserved subarea council meets skeptical reaction to a certificate of need it favors in a regional facilities review committee. According to a study of the HSAs in federal Region X, which includes the states of Alaska, Washington, Oregon, and Idaho, even in agencies where the councils do not dominate the HSA, "these bodies are exercising a great deal of influence on the review process. HSAs appear to be extremely sensitive to pressure from their subareas."[24]

In sum, the central management task of HSA leadership is neither comprehensive planning nor negotiating agreements among members of the HSA board; it is developing and staffing the three-part organizational structure and then reconciling the distinctive contributions of its subunits —institution-oriented committees, plan-oriented staff, and area-oriented subarea councils. The complexity of organization-building takes a great deal of time—time ironically diverted from the planning enterprise. Almost five years after passage of the planning law, a survey of Region X

23. *Health Planning and Resources Development Amendments of 1979*, H. Rept. 96-190, 96 Cong. 1 sess. (Government Printing Office, 1979), p. 36.
24. Lawson, "Evaluation of the Performance of HSA's in Region X," p. 11.

HSAs found that "most of the agencies have been more concerned with internal problems and meeting designation deadlines than with their relationships to the external environment."[25] As a result, plans have often been rushed and superficial. Delays in the federal bureaucracy in issuing regulations and guidelines addressing these internal questions are partly to blame. But one should not infer from this that more time and guidance will make the plans deliberative and profound. As these organizational structures become articulated, entrenched, and committed, tensions and clashes of viewpoint may become more frequent. The management task is largely one of negotiating and keeping peace among internal subunits. The plan is largely a "resultant" of internal organizational politics.

The HSA in Its State and Local Environment

The second structural question about health planning concerns the HSA's ability to exert *interorganizational* influence, that is, its success in getting its work (plan, decision, advice, whatever) taken seriously by other organizations in the health care field at the local and state levels. The United States has never looked favorably on master or central planning bodies with strong powers. Therefore, planners are often charged with developing a plan whose precise uses in shaping the larger world of public policy are ambiguous. The influence of planning agencies tends to lie not in clear lines of authority but in interorganizational networks of persuasion and interest. The HSAs are no exception. As one federal official said: "The annual implementation plan must be the *community's* work plan. The HSA by itself can't do a damn thing."

In theory HSAs should be of major interest to other health regulatory bodies. For example, HSA "appropriateness" reviews and data and analyses about the institutional needs of an area might help the professional standards review organizations (PSROs) put their norms for medical treatment in context. Instead of simply assuming that prevailing practice patterns are right and proper, an HSA-PSRO dialogue would ask whether these patterns are in fact appropriate under alternative institutional assumptions, for example, fewer beds here or an ambulatory surgical center there. These are questions the PSROs themselves tend not to pursue.

Again, CON staffs in the SHPDAs might be expected to depend heavily on HSA deliberations on the need for hospitals and other institutional

25. Ibid., p. 14.

alternatives, for the staffs are often too few and too burdened with the details of particular cases to take a broad view of community needs. The same may be said of state rate-setters, who typically examine individual hospital budgets or categories of budgets and have neither the time nor the mandate to address broad questions about the community's needs for various types and mixes of services. In all these areas the "big picture" supplied by HSAs should fill important gaps and give more narrowly focused regulators greater insight into the roots and ramifications of their work. In practice, however, HSAs have not yet exerted much influence on these agencies. There are several reasons.

HSA Difficulties

It is to be expected that the demand for the products of HSAs will bear some relation to the perceived quality and usefulness of what the HSAs supply. However, for reasons set out above—in particular the strains of establishing and then running a generalist organization that must specialize sufficiently to address a very broad, diverse, and complex mission—many HSAs remain mired in their own formation and maintenance problems and therefore have been unable to produce careful, useful, and pointed plans. The quality of plans differs from place to place, but few would deny that some HSA plans are little more than laundry lists of projects, wish lists of general "priorities" and "emphases," or compendia of updated CHP planning exercises. Frequently the plans do not achieve a level of specificity that carries clear implications for the daily tasks of more focused regulators, and even when they do, these regulators (for example, PSROs, SHPDA staffs, and hospital rate-setters) often have methods and ideas of their own, quite different from those of the HSA.

Organizational Definition of Role and Mission

PSROs have had little use (at least to date) for HSA thoughts on the relationship between institutional needs and local norms governing hospital use. Most of the reasons derive from the different ways in which the organizations define their "distinctive competence."[26] For one thing, most of the questions of central interest to the HSAs fall outside the basic PSRO man-

26. The terms "definition of role and mission" and "distinctive competence" come from Philip Selznick, *Leadership in Administration* (Harper and Row, 1957), p. 42 and chap. 3.

date, which does not direct PSROs to speculate about systems change but to monitor the care of patients covered by certain federal programs. Moreover, the PSROs view themselves as professional peer groups monitoring, educating, and disciplining peers; their workings are an intraprofessional affair and publicity is abhorrent to them. The HSAs, by contrast, are multiconstituency bodies that pride themselves on openness, participation, and publicity. PSROs have therefore been unwilling to release to HSAs, or to other onlookers, information naming particular hospitals, doctors, and patients. Even apart from their "duty" of confidentiality, PSROs view themselves as an elite with a monopoly on the interpretation of the medical information they gather. One observer summarized their view as follows: "Even if PSRO data went to HSAs, who'd know how to use them? Very few. It's a slow process of education. Having unskilled, undiplomatic planners using complex data about providers for their own purposes is not necessarily in the public interest." In sum, the HSAs and PSROs have very different organizational characters—the one is a broad-gauged planning body, the other a highly focused monitoring body; one is a public, participatory forum, the other a mode of professional self-regulation—and these distinctions set limits on the degree of coordination they seek.

Relations between state rate-setting agencies and HSAs offer another example of the limits that diversity of organizational mission imposes on coordination. The approaches of the two bodies to hospitals often diverge sharply: the HSA's findings about the community's "need" for hospital beds and facilities of one type or another have little concrete bearing on such quite distinct questions as whether the charges of a hospital are reasonably related to its costs of doing business and whether or not that hospital is efficiently run. Moreover, HSA decision processes may seem to be offensively soft and political to the hard-nosed economists who staff or run many rate-setting bodies. The clearest case in point is Maryland, where officials of the state Health Services Cost Review Commission have often publicly blasted the HSAs in their state for refusing to be tough and "economical" in their planning recommendations. The problem appears to be reduced when rate-setters have some planning background and HSAs assign a prominent role to economists on their staffs. However, when HSAs with relatively little economic expertise confront rate-setting bodies dominated by self-confident economists, interagency relations are apt to be chilly.

Bureaucratic Turf

The HSA mission is much closer to that of CON officials than it is to that of PSROs or rate-setters. The need assessments integral to the HSA planning process are expected to provide an analytical foundation for CON decisions, and CON offices are required by the planning law to take account of HSA recommendations. One might therefore expect to find rather close cooperation between the two agencies. HSA–CON agency relations differ significantly from state to state. At the risk of overgeneralizing, however, there appear to be two broad patterns of interaction. First, the state may largely stand aside from HSA deliberations on certificates of need and rubber stamp the work of the HSA. Second, the state may (in the almost identical words of observers interviewed in two different states) let the HSAs do all the hard review work while reserving the actual decision for itself. The former pattern appears to be common among states that came relatively late to a CON program.[27] Where HSAs preceded or grew up alongside the CON program, they may keep strong hands on the process. In states that adopted CON programs well before the passage of the planning law, however, the second pattern is evident. In these states well-developed and entrenched CON staffs may resent Johnnies-come-lately invading their turf, upsetting their procedures, and adding new and seemingly uninformed voices to their reviews. That the HSA position on a proposed certificate of need may be the result of deference to an assertive subarea council or of a temporary truce between a council and a facilities review committee does not increase the CON staff's confidence in HSA planning. And the localism of the HSA reviews may aggravate their fears. HSAs generally learn that they accomplish more by negotiating with would-be CON applicants early and informally at preapplication stages than by intervening later and facing a choice between acquiescence and public battling after the application has been submitted. Therefore, the HSA may preempt consultation between the applicant and the CON staff, may make representations about the likelihood and terms of approval that contradict the CON staff's preferences, and may be allied with the applicant at later (that is, state-level) stages of review. For these reasons, the CON staff may be reluctant to share "real" decisionmaking power with the HSAs.

Moreover, even if the HSA establishes harmonious relations with the CON staff, fragmentation of planning and regulatory activities in some

27. When the health planning law was enacted in 1974 about half the states had CON laws.

states can leave important decision points unaffected. In Massachusetts, for example, "the state health plan is prepared by the Office of State Health Planning, CON reviews are performed by the Determination of Need Office, and CON decisions are made by the Public Health Council."[28] The more fragmented the CON authority is at the state level, the more numerous are the institutions with which the HSA must attempt to coordinate, and the more frequent are the opportunities for clashes over bureaucratic turf.[29]

These observations suggest the counterintuitive hypothesis that long state experience with health care regulation is not necessarily a precursor or predictor of smooth adaptation to *federal* planning and regulatory programs. Quite the contrary, new federal bodies may find less hospitality and coordination in states with a relatively long history of regulation—and the bureaucracies this implies—than in latecomers. Although early regulatory efforts indicate a greater *willingness* to regulate, the practical problem of meshing entrenched state bureaucracies with recently devised federal planning and regulatory agencies is not dispelled by a general consistency of mission.

Financing and Grant Patterns

It would seem intuitively obvious that an organization charged with comprehensive planning for the needs and resources of its jurisdiction must have some control, or at any rate leverage, over decisions about those needs and resources if its plans are to carry weight. But the fragmentation and heterogeneity of health insurance financing and grant-in-aid patterns in the United States place major elements of the needs-resources relationship beyond the HSAs' influence, let alone control. HSAs may express their opinions about the optimal numbers and distribution of physicians by specialty and place within their regions, but they can do little to influence the location and specialization decisions of physicians or the flow of federal manpower grants and loans to medical schools and students. They can do little to affect the big decisions about health benefits and premiums, which take place mainly in collective bargaining in the private sector. Medicare and medicaid are entitlement programs, the one guaranteeing federal aid

28. Codman Report, p. 76.
29. On problems of coordination arising from multiple clearance points, see Jeffrey Pressman and Aaron Wildavsky, *Implementation* (University of California Press, 1973), especially chap. 5.

to the elderly, the other to the poor, for a range of medical services set forth in law. Furthermore, according to one HSA statement, "the present method of reimbursement" in these programs "overshadows most local efforts at cost containment."[30] Resentful about alleged HSA discrimination against them, health maintenance organizations have fought free of much of the CON process.[31] Finally, as noted above, such federal regulatory efforts as PSROs and such state efforts as rate-setting are usually far removed institutionally from health planning. In sum, in the words of Katharine G. Bauer: "The Planning Act excludes from the purview of the agencies it creates most of the key elements that currently determine the way the U.S. health system actually operates."[32]

The general point is a familiar one to organizational analysts: that two or more agencies labor in related fields and might in theory reap advantages from close cooperation does not automatically produce coordination.[33] A number of intervening organizational variables should be given careful consideration: one agency's ability to supply a product in demand by another, the agencies' definitions of their roles and missions, the sense of bureaucratic turf and priority, and administrative arrangements dividing fund flows between the public and private sectors and among levels of government. For these and other reasons, interorganizational relations between HSAs and other health regulatory agencies will probably remain spotty.

HSAs and the Federal Government

For better or worse, the HSAs have not been left alone to founder in their intraorganizational and interorganizational difficulties. HSAs are, after all, federal creatures, and the federal government, notably the Health Resources Administration (HRA) in the Department of Health and Human Services has an organizational interest of its own in their success. As planning officials in the ten federal regions contemplate their charges' pro-

30. "Statement of the Florida Gulf Health System Agency on Consumer Participation in Health Planning," presented to the Committee on Health Planning Goals and Standards of the Institute of Medicine, National Academy of Sciences, Washington, D.C., March 27, 1980, p. 3.

31. P.L. 96-79, sec. 1527.

32. Katharine G. Bauer, *Cost Containment under PL 93-641: Strengthening the Partnership between Health Planning and Regulation*, Report Series R58-8 (Harvard University Center for Community Health and Medical Care, January 1978), p. 29.

33. See ibid. for an extensive discussion of these problems in the programs discussed here.

gress to date, problems are evident and frustrations numerous. Some officials interviewed for this study were harshly frank. To summarize a frequently encountered critique: HSAs were created in 1974, often have had the benefit of building on CHP foundations, receive hundreds of thousands (or more) of federal dollars annually, and have sizable staffs—and have done little more than assemble some warmed-over, highly general, and banal "plans" of little practical use to anyone. If the program is to shape up into a success, the regions need specific success stories to hold before HRA eyes in the central office, before secretarial eyes in the Department of Health and Human Services, and before congressional, General Accounting Office, Office of Management and Budget, and White House eyes. (The need for dramatic success stories grew very urgent indeed in 1981 when the Reagan administration took office and promptly proposed to eliminate the federal health planning program.) But how are such successes to be produced? Federal officials can exert little direct influence on outcomes; the only promising point of leverage is the plan itself. As the program has developed, central office regulations and guidelines, and therefore regional office instructions and pressures, have been imposed in an attempt to discipline the planning process; to require and coax the locals to make the plans more specific, rigorous, and quantitative; and then, in their CON and PUFF decisions, to follow the logic of the plan wherever it may lead. In this way, it is hoped, the planning process can be made to show "a demonstrable difference."[34]

In HSA eyes, however, federal rules and guidelines are at once offensively specific and unhelpfully vague. The locals correctly suspect that the feds have no better ideas about how to write health plans than they themselves do, and they therefore resent federal efforts to force an artificial consensus. Nevertheless, under the hot breath of quantifying overseers, the feds have no choice but to insist, and the locals, eager to get their plans (and next year's grant award) approved with minimum conflict have no choice but to try to comply, or to seem to.

As one might expect, these downward pressures set off a complex chain reaction within the organizational structures of the HSA. Told by the feds to go back to the drawing board and improve their section of the plan, committees often grumble that a supposedly local planning process is being emasculated by domineering bureaucrats. At the same time, the pressure tends to strengthen the hands of the staff members, who are the repositories

34. Cain and Darling, "Health Planning in the United States," p. 23.

of methodological sophistication and therefore of specificity, quantification, and rigor, and quite often are the only ones who appear to understand
the mumbo-jumbo the agency has been told to master. But when providers
on the committees, subarea councils, or board then "test" the staff's proposed methodologies and quantified planning criteria against their own
situations and institutional interests, they quickly identify distasteful results (for instance, a ward to be closed or not to be renovated after all) and
with much noise and animation expose all the absurdities and anomalies of
the mindless application of a general method or formula to an obviously
exceptional case like their own. Letters from locals (angry) and feds (po-
lite, reassuring, but firm) go back and forth. A federal regional planning
expert or team is dispatched to meet with the staff, executive director, and
perhaps a few interested board members in order to help them understand
"how to do it." The HSAs are given to understand that the content of their
plans is theirs to define as they see fit, at least within broad limits. But
whatever they do, they must do it rigorously and specifically; the plan must
be studded with numbers, formulas, criteria, standards, and perhaps even a
few equations.

The HSA staff and committee members then meet to thrash out a com-
promise that will be more specific than what had been contemplated before
but still hedged and ambiguous enough to be tolerable. The feds withdraw,
knowing that they have bought all the rigor the local political market can
produce. Plans that seem better than the norm are called to HRA attention; the agencies that wrote them attract "close interest." Top Department
of Health and Human Services officials reassure the Office of Management
and Budget and Congress that the planning process is coming along, that
many costs (including the time and effort of local notables) have been sunk,
and that after all there really is no alternative to local grass roots democracy when one wants cost containment but abhors bureaucracy and government regulation. Even as they receive their appropriations, however, these
officials worry that the budget-minded skeptics will prevail next time; are
acutely aware of the importance of quickly producing large, tangible (that
is, quantifiable) results, especially savings; and increase pressure on the
regions to find such evidence. Regional pressures for specificity, rigor, and
measurement are in turn stepped up, and HSAs again respond by putting
their staffs, committees, and subarea councils on the trail of compromises
that quantify for the sake of quantification, that is, for the sake of feds.

The Mythical Foundations of Health Planning: A Critique

The central problem with the HSA effort is that it rests on theoretical foundations that cannot properly be institutionalized, that is, embodied in structures that effectively relate the planning strategy to the goals it is intended to achieve. What explains these structural difficulties? What assumptions and promises led the federal designers of the health planning program to invent institutional arrangements expected to do so much yet equipped to do so little? Three theoretical assumptions—which might be termed consumer-dominated pluralism, self-regulating localism, and scientifically grounded planning—are especially problematic.

Consumer-Dominated Pluralism

Cain and Darling write:

> One of the fundamental assumptions on which this . . . program is based is that a community of interest, a set of shared perspectives, can be developed between consumers and providers, insurance carriers and policy holders, employers and employees, town and gown, in the health sector. Out of these shared perspectives, it is assumed Health Systems Plans—and regulatory decisions—can emerge. . . . To develop such shared perspectives, all interests are to be represented on the planning agency boards—a majority of consumers, to be sure, but an effective minority of providers as well. . . .[35]

The HSAs are to provide a forum in which diverse social interests—divergent enough to be distinct and even conflictual but not so divergent as to be beyond reason and reconciliation—may come together and reach compromises in the general public interest. "Provider dominance," ever-feared and ever-impending, is to be checked by provisions for a board with a majority of consumers. Unfortunately balance cannot be so easily mandated. Consumer-dominated pluralism puts an excessive burden on consumers, demanding that they walk a tightrope, neither deferring to providers nor becoming so adversarial as to cease being constructive. Somewhere between capitulation and intractability lies the proper consumer role. Alas, no one knows what this mythical terrain looks like.

Although evidence is accumulating on what those occupying consumer roles do, little is known about how consumers perceive and evaluate the health care system.[36] It is therefore far from clear that many consumers

---

35. Ibid., p. 21.
36. In general, public opinion polls offer the rather unhelpful findings that the citizenry is quite satisfied with the U.S. health care system but nonetheless is worried about its costs,

believe in and are able to define and articulate a consumer interest in health care clearly and distinctly different from the interests of providers. That consumers will often take the lead in saying no to expansion-minded providers in the name of regulatory efficiency and cost containment is highly doubtful. Consumer participants, like other Americans, want to be "constructive," not "negative," and they soon find that the identification and elaboration of unmet needs and the laying of plans to meet them is far more gratifying than assaulting or undoing the plans of valued community health resources such as hospitals. According to Basil Mott, "the HSAs, like the CHP agencies, will probably have their greatest programmatic effect in encouraging and assisting the development of desirable new programs. It is easier to identify and agree on unmet needs and to assist needed program development, especially when resources are available, than to change or discontinue already existing programs."[37] In the words of the Consumer Coalition for Health: "Most consumers enter health planning with an eye turned toward specific issues: access, quality, or more humane institutional alternatives."[38]

Consumer energies find four main outlets. First, prevention, wellness, health education, health promotion, holistic medicine, and the need to encourage these and other fashionable movements stand high among the priorities of many consumers. Providers may privately snicker at these enthusiasms, but they know that by joining in these "promotions" they can win goodwill and allies in the fights that count.

Second, consumers often emphasize relatively neglected and low-technology services—mental health counseling, hypertension and diabetes management, prematernity and postmaternity care for mothers and children, and the like. That improving these services may raise health care budgets, at least in the short run, is thought secondary.

Third, consumers may assail or try to block various evils that local institutions have perpetrated. For example, the Consumer Coalition for Health boasted of an HSA that "unearthed mammoth abuses and scandalous profit-making by a dialysis company," of another that "discovered that

---

access, manpower, and the like; that many citizens favor national health insurance in general but not any one proposal in particular; and so forth. The polls furnish no basis at all for judging how public opinion would address the central practical policy problem, making trade-offs among "goods."

37. Mott, "The New Health Planning System," p. 251. See, however, the Codman Report, pp. 54–61, or Altman, "The Policy of Health Care Regulation," pp. 573–76, for the view that the HSAs are doing more regulation than expected.

38. Consumer Coalition for Health, "Written Submission," p. 5.

a local hospital was building massage parlors for its doctors and charging it off to consumers, third-party payers, and Medicaid and Medicare," and of another that investigated pharmacy pricing and uncovered kickbacks to local doctors.[39] Hospitals that fail to meet their obligations to medicaid recipients or to provide enough free care are another favored target. Institutions with expansion plans that entail demolition of or eviction from homes in adjacent neighborhoods arc still another. In these cases, consumers may become skilled at using the regulatory leverage of the HSA—especially the CON review process—to bargain for institutional "reforms."

It is difficult to evaluate these reforms because they have not been studied closely and dispassionately. They may arise from indefensible pressure applied by uninformed and power-hungry citizens to administrators trying to do a good job in trying circumstances. They may bring about overdue correction of institutional indifference and neglect and may enhance the altruism and moral fiber of local providers. Be this as it may, they have little to do with cost containment.

Finally, consumers show some interest in cost containment. Sometimes this interest reflects their determination to punish a recalcitrant institution. Sometimes it reflects a generalized hostility toward high-technology medicine. Sometimes it reflects staff influence and sometimes a sincere commitment to a more efficient and cost-effective health care system. Approaches to "costing" based on a thoroughgoing assessment of resources in light of needs are seldom to be found, however. For one thing, thc issues involved—which (to recall the consumer statement quoted earlier) require "a merry chase through HSPs, AIPs, square footage formulae, and debt ratios, etc." —are boring, dry, and time-consuming. For another, consumers do not wish to see their area lose ground in the competition for good health care resources any more than providers do. Consumers are not, of course, indifferent to waste and inefficiency and most have grasped that bedrock of American health planning, Roemer's law.[40] But Roemer's law, which in essence holds that a bed built is a bed filled and which thercfore seems to point to constraints on or reductions in bed capacity as a main route to cost containment, states a *general* relationship, whereas HSA decisions are exercises in the analysis of highly particular, indeed seemingly unique, cir-

39. Ibid.
40. This "law" is named after Milton I. Roemer, who postulated it in "Bed Supply and Hospital Utilization: A Natural Experiment," *Hospitals*, vol. 35 (November 1, 1961), pp. 36–42.

cumstances.[41] Direction is even more lacking in decisionmaking about technology, for which, as Louise Russell has remarked, there is no Roemer's law.[42] Health planning confronts an unending parade of priorities; health regulation faces an equally populous parade of exceptional cases. This combination of unlimited need-listing and indulgent exception-making does not conform to the clash of distinctive interests pictured by the "countervailing power" model of HSAs.

Even when consumers are inclined to get tough with providers, the organizational setting in which they must press their case is rarely conducive to persistence. In the HSA committees and subarea councils, providers, worried about their own institutions, precedents, or "logs" soon to be rolled are much more likely to attend meetings and to participate knowledgeably and fully than are consumers. Four or five providers versus one or two consumers are apt to prove highly persuasive. Those who would employ small groups for planning purposes must abide with the consequences of small-group dynamics. One of these consequences is a tendency for the groups to honor intensity of preferences, to sympathize with those members whose interests are clearly on the line and whose emotions are deeply engaged. These members are often the providers whose institutional excellence or character may be threatened. Another consequence is for community residents who expect to live, socialize, and work together over time to avoid and reduce conflict by means of deference and reciprocity.

It has been pointed out with justifiable celebration in some quarters that despite the pessimism of early critics the HSAs are saying "no" oftener than expected, that they are doing more regulation than predicted, and that consumers have frequently accepted the need for cost containment with surprising dedication. All of this, it is said, represents the triumph of heroic public-spiritedness over the true expansionist interests of local residents. There is no intention here to minimize this public-mindedness. The point of the argument developed here is rather that HSAs are a faulty cost containment mechanism *precisely because* they demand local public-spiritedness in so high a degree.

Vast organizational anguish tends to accompany a negative decision by an HSA on a question of genuine interest to a local health care institution.

41. On the difficulties in the way of rigorous application of "need" and other criteria to CON reviews, see Harold S. Luft and Gary A. Frisvold, "Decisionmaking in Regional Planning Agencies," *Journal of Health Politics, Policy, and Law*, vol. 4 (Summer 1979), pp. 250–72.

42. Louise B. Russell, *Technology in Hospitals: Medical Advances and Their Diffusion* (Brookings Institution, 1979), p. 140.

The many hours of negotiation; the recurrent cycle of justification and critique; the charges of lay ignorance on one side and of provider dominance on another; the endless fiddling with formulas and ratios no one understands; the contrived public hearings at which a hospital displays its audiovisual aids to testify to the urgent needs of a venerated community institution and "the community" in attendance (three-fourths of it employed by or related to employees of the hospital) rises in long-winded support; the 4–3 vote finally taken at 1 A.M. in committee; the endless buttonholing and handholding; the threat of appeal and legal redress; all of this, inherent in self-regulating localism, raises the personal and organizational costs of nay-saying very high. Few care to go through this process very often. One may give the HSAs (especially their consumers and staffs) the credit they richly deserve for their firmness and still conclude that a local, highly participatory body is not the best means of making cost-containing decisions and that nay-saying would be more reliably (though no more easily) institutionalized at higher levels of the federal system.

Moreover, consumers determined to fight for such cost-containing measures as denied expansion or modernization projects or for mergers or closures, may find that their success in persuading the HSA board carries little weight in the larger community. Tough HSA recommendations often come under sharp fire at public meetings from contingents of "average citizens," some speaking out spontaneously, others orchestrated by providers,[43] and HSAs often back down under such fire. In short, cost-conscious *consumer representatives* may find themselves at odds with the sentiments of *community participants*—a predicament given too little thought by enthusiasts of "greater consumer representation and participation."[44]

It is unreasonable to mark out an independent and separate consumer role and then expect consumers to conform to it. Such a role is, at bottom, contrived and inauthentic. Abstract and systemic health consumers are nowhere to be found. People consume health care in a variety of very definite social contexts with logics of their own—for example, as head of a family worried about the health of a loved one; as a community resident who is concerned about the distance to and quality of hospital care should need arise; as a taxpayer and wage earner considering the size of a payroll deduction or of a wage increase forgone; as a more or less informed layman contemplating the implications of some new technology (or the implica-

43. Codman Report, pp. 61–67.
44. See Bruce C. Vladeck, "Health Planning—Participation and Its Discontents," *American Journal of Public Health*, vol. 69 (April 1979), pp. 331–32.

tions of the writings of Ivan Illich); as personalities with certain attitudes toward risk, pain, and one's own body; or as members of local organizations such as unions, churches, hospital boards, and auxiliaries involved with health care institutions. There is no pure consumer role; even the most resolutely skeptical citizen is compromised by emotions and identifications that inhibit political self-definition as a countervailing power to providers. (There are of course "professional consumers" in the "Naderite" sense. But in practice the role usually entails a deeper and more consistent antagonism toward providers than most consumers are willing to adopt.)[45] Because the HSA effort shares a central fallacy about the consumer in current health policy analysis—the determination to "decontextualize" him, to reduce him to pure *payer*— it expects him to define and articulate a set of interests distinct from those of the paid, the providers. Unsurprisingly, consumers continually violate these expectations, leaving their advocates fuming about provider dominance.

The unhappy fact is that there is no more agreement about the nature and purposes of the consumer role in health planning than there is about the nature and purposes of health planning itself. At least six distinct roles envisioned for consumer representatives may be culled from the literature and from legislative documents and debates. First, the representative role may be to express the community's viewpoint. A second role is to express the views of unrepresented or underrepresented minorities or disadvantaged elements in the community. A third is to oppose—that is, countervail—the provider perspective. A fourth is to supplement—or perhaps supplant—the positions of political officials. A fifth is to represent the stands of organizational constituencies. A sixth is to speak for those with special health care needs.

The various roles imply different recruitment procedures. The first, for example, would seem to call for a general election of consumers; the second and sixth for quotas of different community strata; the third and fourth for deliberate recruitment of those with distinct policy views (antiprovider and antipolitician, respectively); and the fifth for selection from among members or officers of formal organizations. And even if agreement about the proper meaning and method of recruitment of consumer representatives could be secured, the equally difficult problem of the relationship between

45. Consumer representatives may empathize with a health care consultant who recounted his "worst nightmare": he is addressing a body of local physicians, flailing them verbally for the waste and inefficiency of fee-for-service medicine, only to be stricken in midsentence with a heart attack and then to be saved by members of his audience.

consumer representation and community participation would remain to be resolved. How legitimate are recommendations or decisions made by consumer representatives on the HSA board but strongly opposed by consumer participants in the community itself?

It is idle to believe that the "proper" composition of HSA boards can be deduced from ever more sophisticated and refined philosophical, legal, and linguistic explications of the concept "consumer." The concept yields no such treasures. If the question at hand is whether, say, working-class persons, or working-class Latinos, or working-class Latinos in need of kidney dialysis should be represented on the HSA board, then this question should be debated on its moral and political merits, not mired in linguistic analysis. "Socially descriptive" representation is a particularly weak solution to the representation puzzle. In local health decisionmaking, representatives should represent their constituencies' *attitudes* (preferences), not merely their *attributes*. And one cannot directly infer attitudes from attributes. Many cleavages cut across such strata as class, race, neighborhood, ethnicity, health status, and so forth. Just as it was demeaning when the federal government incorporated in Great Society programs participation provisions based on the view that "the poor" and "the black community" are homogeneous, so too it is demeaning to assume that on health issues Latinos (or whomever) must be homogeneous in interest and attitude and may therefore be adequately represented by any Latino.

The familiar alternative—selecting consumer representatives from among the members or officers of consumer organizations—is no more clearly preferable, however. As Checkoway notes, consumer activism and organization in the health field do not conform to the traditional image of political mobilization boiling up from grievances deeply and widely felt in the community. Rather, the planning program itself and its institutional resources "have helped create career opportunities and support networks among activists and professionals seeking to identify issues and build organizations in a field in which consumers typically lack awareness of inequalities in the delivery of services, or do not accept health planning as a community problem, or show little support for consumer intervention."[46] This suggests the need for skepticism about whom and what self-proclaimed consumer groups represent. It is understandable that such groups argue that "to become responsible and responsive representatives, consumers need the technical and political support of an organized consumer health

46. Checkoway, "Consumer Movements in Health Planning," p. 180.

constituency,"[47] because wide acceptance of this view serves their organizational maintenance needs. There is a natural tension between socially descriptive representatives, especially elected and other prominent group figures, and organizational representatives over the "right" to speak for the consumer. Neither side is right; the representative limitations of both sides should be recognized.

Finally, notwithstanding the program designers' dim view of state and local politicians, one should ask what representative roles *these* figures properly play in health planning. Obviously participation is in some sense a good thing in, indeed a defining feature of, a democracy, but a democracy is a hierarchy or polyarchy of diverse representative structures. Therefore, the general case for representation and participation implies nothing at all about the specific case for one or another approach to representation in health care policy. This point is usually ignored in discussions about consumer representation, which seem to assume that because participation is good, one cannot have too much of it and that no proposal that appears to increase it can legitimately be faulted. Yet the issue remains: the community has representatives—elected officials—and it may be unwise to forget them or usurp their roles or complicate their lives without first giving careful attention to the character of the polyarchy one creates by devising such supplementary, or supplanting, structures as the HSAs.

Because there is so little agreement about the content of the representative role, it is doubtful that any of these questions can be answered sensibly in the detailed language of statute, regulation, or court decision. Therefore, the present drift toward ever more detailed statutory, administrative, and judicial embroidery on the "true meaning" of consumer representation is unfortunate. The long and often unhappy history of similar efforts in urban policy—where requirements were diluted from "maximum feasible participation" in the community action program to "widespread citizen participation" in the model cities program to an "adequate opportunity to participate" in the community development block grant program—could teach health planners the futility of the search for uniform, correct, and precise definitions in this area and may strengthen the case for increasing the discretion of the states and of the HSAs themselves in designing their consumer representation structures.[48]

47. Ibid., p. 178.

48. On the Office of Equal Opportunity experience, see Daniel P. Moynihan, *Maximum Feasible Misunderstanding* (Free Press, 1970). On model cities, see Lawrence D. Brown and Bernard J. Frieden, "Rulemaking by Improvisation: Guidelines and Goals in the Model Cities

European practice offers some instructive contrasts with the American approach to consumer-dominated pluralism. In continental Europe consumers are represented neither by socially descriptive figures nor by self-constituted consumer organizations but by organizations, the sickness funds, whose business it is to *purchase* health care. In West Germany, for example, most of the population is enrolled in occupation-related sickness funds. There are more than 1,000 separate funds, which compete to some extent—that is, within the constraints of legally required benefit packages —for members, especially for better-off and low-risk members. To retain their members, their reputations, and the better risks, the funds must offer an attractive package (extra benefits, perceived quality, attractive facilities, and so on) at rates that do not outrage the subscriber. (In West Germany half the cost of coverage is paid by the employee and half by the employer.) The funds must therefore bargain with physician organizations and with hospitals over fees and rates and have developed large, expert staffs that match those of the provider organizations in analytic and technical skill.[49] The skills, numbers, and continuity of the sickness fund bureaucracies supply the specialized leverage that consumer representatives in the United States generally lack. Moreover, in Germany the workers' sickness funds, which enroll almost half the population, have close historical ties to

Program," *Policy Sciences,* vol. 7 (December 1976), pp. 455–88, especially pp. 464–74. The language quoted from the Housing and Community Development Act of 1974 appears in P.L. 93-383, sec. 104.

There are many striking similarities between the model cities program and the planning effort: the emphasis on planning and coordination; the determination to pursue them by means of a newly built local organization; the deep concern with citizen participation; the federal attempt to make the planners follow a rigorous sequence of goal-setting, problem analysis, and so on, resulting in long- and short-term plans; the problems of reconciling the powers of the new organization with those of local public officials and with the interests of local organizations, both public and private; and more. Unfortunately academicians and public officials have apparently made little effort to learn from the difficulties of the model cities program lessons of practical advantage to the HSAs. See Lawrence D. Brown, "Coordination of Federal Urban Policy: Organizational Politics in Three Model Cities" (Ph.D. dissertation, Harvard University, 1973).

49. On Europe, see William A. Glaser, *Health Insurance Bargaining: Foreign Lessons for Americans* (New York: Gardner Press, 1978); Howard M. Leichter, *A Comparative Approach to Policy Analysis: Health Care Policy In Four Nations* (New York: Cambridge University Press, 1979), especially chaps. 5 and 6; and Jan Blanpain and others, *National Health Insurance and Health Resources: The European Experience* (Harvard University Press, 1978.) As Glaser notes, Germany is unique in Europe in allowing "differences among funds in benefits to the subscriber and in payments to doctors for the same benefits" (p. 221). Even in the absence of such competition, however, the funds' wish to assure their mass membership that subscribers get a good value for their money gives them an organizational incentive to represent the consumer in bargaining with providers.

the labor unions and the (now ruling) Social Democratic Party. These groups are a potentially powerful legislative coalition that did in fact come together successfully in 1977 to pass a cost containment law.[50] Even so, the adequacy of consumer representation lies very much in the eye of the beholder, and one recent account describes its condition in the German health care system as "bleak."[51]

It is doubtful that one can do much better, however, and it is clear that the United States cannot now go even this far toward institutionalized consumer representation. In the United States the sickness funds (Blue Cross and commercial insurance companies) often represent providers or shareholders more than consumers, a consequence of the circumstances of the birth and maintenance of these organizations.[52] In the United States historical ties among "progressive" parties, unions, and insurers are largely absent too. It is therefore not surprising that the United States tries to achieve consumer representation by mandating and designating consumer representatives on planning boards. But it is also not surprising that this approach encounters many obstacles.

Some believe that European negotiating patterns contain a clear structural lesson for the United States: instead of trying to spin from whole cloth new consumer representation bodies, policymakers should bring purchasers of care more directly into decisions about health care rates and charges. This recommendation has several problems, two of which will be briefly noted here. First, the fragmentation of the U.S. insurance industry complicates representation in bargaining. It is difficult to imagine how Blue Cross, Blue Shield, private companies, health maintenance organizations, union plans, medicare, medicaid, and still others could come together in the equivalent of an association of sickness funds with leadership speaking authoritatively for all members. Second, the decentralization of health care regulation in the United States further complicates the issue. Presumably much of the bargaining would occur at the state level, where the review and setting of hospital rates and the regulation of health insurance take place. It will do the insurers little good to strike a bargain with providers if there is no assurance that state regulators (rate-setters, CON reviewers, and

50. See Deborah Stone, "Health Care Cost Containment in West Germany," *Journal of Health Policy, Politics, and Law,* vol. 4 (Summer 1979), pp. 176–99; and William A. Glaser, "Politics of Cost Control Abroad," *Bulletin of the New York Academy of Medicine,* vol. 56 (January-February 1980), pp. 107–14.

51. Blainpan and others, *National Health Insurance and Health Resources,* pp. 41–42.

52. See Herman M. Somers and Anne R. Somers, *Doctors, Patients, and Health Insurance* (Brookings Institution, 1961), chaps. 14–16.

others) will abide by it. Moreover, if the weaker insurance interests in a state suspect that their larger and more powerful brethren have cut a deal with state regulators at their expense, bargaining may break down. In short, European negotiating structures presuppose a national health insurance program and a national health insurance statute that imposes some unifying structure on the organization of the negotiating parties, on the nature of the bargaining process, and on the allowable limits of subnational diversity.

Although the structural and organizational preconditions of a disciplined, integrated pluralism in the health field are not met here, the United States must nonetheless try to make pluralism work. The American medical and political systems are extremely fragmented. Many interests are inescapably involved in health care policy, and some means must be found to bring them together on common ground. In Europe, where health care financing takes place subject to public law and sometimes with public funds, it is much easier for governments to convene negotiations and to keep participants at the table. The elements of the system come together in "health insurance bargaining" between sickness funds and providers, with unions, employers, government, and other interested and highly organized parties standing on the sidelines watching and prepared to influence and perhaps even countermand the agreements of the two principal negotiators.[53] The U.S. health care system, by contrast, is largely private, and even in much of its public sector it has chosen to purchase care by cost- and charge-based retrospective reimbursement methods, not by means of rates set forth prospectively in fee schedules. With arrangements so heterogeneous and decentralized, the United States must experiment with heterogeneous and decentralized frameworks for negotiation. The HSAs take halting steps in this direction by establishing forums that bring major interests into negotiations over the contents of the health plan.

Bargaining, however, is not a panacea. Creating forums in which providers and payers (on behalf of consumers) come together to negotiate is only half the job. The other half is the establishment of government rules and procedures that constrain bargaining, that is, set financial or other limits within which agreement must remain. The art of designing a workable negotiation system lies in finding the right balance between constraining structures imposed by government and bargaining autonomy enjoyed by

53. "Health insurance bargaining" is the title of the Glaser book cited in note 49.

providers and payers. This balance shifts with time and circumstance and must be intermittently modified.

In Europe negotiations do not center on the design of a comprehensive plan to address all facets of the health care system but on a tangible and immediate financial question, the reimbursement levels for acts contained in the fee schedule. This in turn implies deliberation on the sources and definition of increases in the cost of medical and hospital practice, on the amount by which mandated contributions can be raised for employers and employees, and more. The structure of and participants in the bargaining process are prescribed in some detail by law, and government usually retains options, such as extending existing fee levels indefinitely or (as in Germany) subjecting the two sides to compulsory arbitration, should negotiations break down.

In recent years health care cost increases have been very high and European governments have modified the structure of negotiations in ways that give them greater leverage. A West German law enacted in 1972, for example, gave the central government a larger role in the planning and financing of hospitals, a field in which the German states have jealously guarded their "rights." A 1976 law created new planning mechanisms to influence the distribution of primary care. The cost containment law of 1977 created, among other central constraints, a multimember concerted action group at the federal level that makes annual recommendations on spending increases. Provider and sickness fund negotiators are expected (though not required) to keep their agreements within this ceiling. Stronger central "constraining structures" are widely seen to be necessary, though perhaps not sufficient, for cost containment.[54]

On occasion European nations resort to localistic round table planning methods. For instance, the West German law of 1976 addressing physician distribution has several points of resemblance to the HSA process.[55] It differs, however, in at least two major respects. First, it aims not at compre-

---

54. Glaser reports, for example: "The trend in the world is toward collective regulation covering entire provinces and entire countries" and toward taking "many essential economic decisions out of the hands of the parties to rate-setting of the individual hospital." Centralization, he notes, is the French solution to regulatory capture: "the financial ministries have the final say, interministerial conferences keep everyone busy preparing the guidelines, and the grassroots regulators are not consulted extensively by the key decision-makers." William A. Glaser, "Paying the Hospital in France" (Center for the Social Sciences, Columbia University, August 1980), pp. XIII-2, XIII-3, XIII-4.

55. Christa Altenstetter and James Warner Bjorkman, "Planning and Implementation: A Comparative Perspective on Health Policy," discussion paper series (International Institute of Management, Wissenschaftszentrum, Berlin, August 1979), p. 27.

hensive planning for the system as a whole but rather at the analysis and cure of a specific problem, physician distribution. Second, it carries the threat of specific sanctions if voluntary methods fail. (The law allows a committee of sickness funds and physician representatives as a last resort to make the establishment of new primary care practices in over-doctored areas contingent on a permit.) No European nation pretends that cost containment can be achieved by means of localistic, vaguely defined participatory processes and neither should the United States.[56]

In Europe as in the United States, the complaint is widespread that providers dominate the negotiating and regulatory processes. It is doubtful, however, that any scheme can be devised in which full-time provider-experts will not somehow dominate part-time consumer-laymen when the two come together to plan for professional concerns. This outcome is a function of widely shared values as much as (probably more than) imbalances of power. The choice lies not between provider and consumer dominance but between various structures and degrees of provider-dominated systems. The reformer's task is to discriminate carefully among these various structures and inquire empirically into their consequences.

Self-Regulating Localism

The creators of the health planning effort assume that assemblies of local interests will regulate their health care demands, acquisitions, and spending if only government will give them a mandate and will subject them to the organizational structures of consumer-dominated pluralism. This assumption is mistaken. Indeed, one might argue that for planning purposes the United States comprises two and only two types of jurisdictions: those with adequate or excellent health resources, which they wish to preserve and enhance; and those that are underserved in some respect and hope to gain more services and resources. The cliché that there is no constituency for cost containment is correct only in part at the federal and state levels; it is by and large quite correct at the local level, however.

The limitations of self-regulating localism are especially evident in the

56. A vignette from Great Britain may be pertinent. When the British Medical Association voted in July 1980 in favor of the abolition of community health councils, "watchdog committees set up in 1974 to represent consumers' interests in the health service," the chairman of the association's general medical services committee argued that they should be retained. He was quoted as saying that "when the Government is hell bent on cuts you need friends. Community health councils have probably done more to preserve local hospitals and local obstetrical units than any other bodies." *The Times* (London), July 11, 1980.

case of hospitals, and not only in the United States. As William Glaser puts it in a report on his research on European approaches to hospital reimbursement:

> One barrier against strict cost control over hospitals is the hesitation of the groups who otherwise are the watchdogs over health spending. The trade unions and sick funds resist higher fees for doctors but give hospitals the benefit of the doubt. The trade unions press for higher wages for hospital employees—the largest component of hospital costs—and oppose shutting small and underused hospitals. Sick funds try to relieve their own financial pressure by getting subsidies from government. Communities would rather have modern hospitals close at hand—even if underused—than save the tax money. Attempts by government to shut hospitals result in community protests and intervention by worried Parliaments, so that budget-cutters and planners often—not always—settle for a compromise. Hospital staffs are learning how to mobilize the community against ceilings on expenditures in particular services. . . .[57]

One explanation of the lack of local taste for self-regulation is that no local actor has any objective interest in trying to limit or take away health resources from his jurisdiction. As Harvey Sapolsky and others have explained, the jurisdictions of those who benefit from community health care resources and of those who pay for them are rarely equivalent.[58] Nor are HSAs obliged to plan within a ceiling, that is, a fixed health budget, so that more of x must mean less or none of y.

More research is needed into the perceptual roots of local indifference to cost containment. Maybe this attitude does indeed reflect the calculated false economizing of "free riders." But perhaps the roots are more subtle. After all, everyone pays for health services in higher premiums, taxes, payroll deductions, prices, and otherwise, and everyone knows it. But just as an attitude of general support for national health insurance or school integration may break down when the supporter is questioned about concrete proposals (the health security plan or the prospect of busing, for instance), so too a general commitment to cost containment may collapse when planners get down to local cases. Every student of budgeting understands this disjunction between general principle and particular applica-

57. William A. Glaser, "Paying the Hospital: Foreign Lessons for the United States (Some Preliminary Conclusions)" (Center for the Social Sciences, Columbia University, December 1979), pp. 6–7.

58. See Harvey M. Sapolsky, "Bottoms Up Is Upside Down," in Institute of Medicine, *Health Planning in the United States*, pp. 131–42, especially pp. 132–33. See also Mancur Olson, Jr., "The Optimal Allocation of Jurisdictional Responsiblity: The Principle of 'Fiscal Equivalence,'" in Subcommittee on Economy in Government of the Joint Economic Committee, *The Analysis and Evaluation of Public Expenditures: The PPB System*, 91 Cong. 2 sess. (GPO, 1969), vol. 1, pp. 321–31.

tion: *of course* less of the federal budget should be spent on health care; but the proper place to make cuts is obviously not the Institutes of Health or medicaid or the Cooperative Health Statistics System, or the health planning program, or. . . .

The response, in other words, depends heavily on how the question is posed. The premise behind self-regulating localism is that central government is the appropriate level at which to pose general questions (about the need for cost containment, for example), but that the local level is the proper site of specific decisionmaking. But the supposedly indispensable insight, the unique wisdom, of local planners about local needs and preferences usually argues for "more and better" or at any rate for no less and no worse. Thus a workable regulatory approach may require reversing the usual premise: central and perhaps state government may need to exploit the abstract and *general* agreement at the local level on the need for cost containment in order to force or constrain *specific* decisions that localities would not voluntarily reach by themselves (that is, apart from steady federal pressure or rules).

It is often argued that visiting the true costs of health services more accurately on those who reap the benefits would lead to cost containment without additional governmental intervention. This could be done in two ways. First, individual approaches seek to make service recipients responsible for more of the health care costs they incur. Second, areal efforts seek to introduce a larger measure of jurisdictional equivalence between communities of those who receive and those who pay for services.

European experience is again suggestive. The West German system, for example, has a high degree of individual targeting of costs: beneficiaries (that is, employees and their dependents) pay half the cost of health care premiums through payroll deductions. In recent years average contribution rates have climbed from about 8.5 percent (1969) to more than 11 percent (1976) of income,[59] yet despite some grumbling no outpouring of popular discontent has occurred nor any major cuts in the very generous benefits Germans enjoy.[60]

59. Klaus-Dirk Henke, "A Short Introduction into the German Health Insurance System" (University of Hanover, West Germany, December 18, 1979), p. 14, table 9.

60. According to Leichter: "The satisfaction and sense of pride expressed by the public, the apparently acceptable level of inequalities, and the generally high level of health and health care indicate that the system is working well. The problem of health care costs must be evaluated in terms of the questions: 'How much is the society willing to pay for health care?' Thus far, Germans and German policy makers appear to be willing to bear rather high costs." (*A Comparative Approach to Policy Analysis*, p. 154.)

Sweden, by contrast, has a high degree of areal cost targeting. Hospitals are supported mainly from county budgets raised by county taxes. Indeed hospitals are by far the largest single item in county tax levies, which would presumably make their costs highly visible and controversial. Yet Swedes on the whole have cheerfully raised county taxes to meet rising hospital costs.[61]

In Germany, Sweden, and elsewhere rapidly rising health care costs have been viewed with alarm mainly by the central government, not by public opinion or localities, and central governments have been the major source of cost containment efforts. This is not surprising: whereas an individual or a locality may evaluate health care costs in a rough and intuitive judgment about whether a payroll deduction or tax bill seems fair enough in light of benefits conferred, central budget-makers must contemplate the extrapolation of present health spending trends to truly horrifying percentages of GNP and of social budgets within a decade or two and must responsibly consider the opportunity costs of health expenditures. The implications are that effective regulation is incompatible with extreme decentralization of the regulatory body; that it is naive to expect more decentralization in the United States to cure problems that decentralization in large measure produces; and that serious efforts at cost containment must come, not from self-regulating local bodies, but from the central or perhaps state government. Of course, the central government must and will involve localities in the design and implementation of cost containment plans, but this involvement presupposes a strong, constraining, centrally established framework. Programs like the HSAs, all involvement and no (or very little) framework, can be expected to accomplish few savings.

Scientifically Grounded Planning

The HSA effort is above all a health *planning* process and the health plans stand at the center of the enterprise. The plans are, so to speak, both output and input: devising plans that are both comprehensive and specific is the first object of the exercise; using those plans to guide regulatory decisions then follows.

Unfortunately the substantive knowledge needed to support plans of great comprehensiveness and specificity in the health care field is lacking.[62] "The agency must consider the array of influences on health," indeed it

---

61. Altenstetter and Bjorkman, "Planning and Implementation," pp. 38–39.
.62. See Bovbjerg, "Problems and Prospects for Health Planning," pp. 93–97 and passim.

must identify "all relevant health factors and problems."[63] These influences, factors, and problems are easy enough to list, but the practical component of the exercise—"where possible isolate those conditions which can be addressed by the delivery system"[64]—is hotly disputed. Equally important, the *relative* contributions of different influences, factors, and problems to health under different conditions are poorly understood.

The same problems beset the instruction that the plan should "describe and characterize the status of the entire health system."[65] If this means making a list of institutions, services, and resources, it is a feasible (though not easy) task. But the second part of the mandate—"noting the effects that changes in one part of the system may have on other parts"[66]—can at best be met with long lists of controverted propositions and counterpropositions; meaning hypotheses or conjectures. Most important, the interactions between the two realms—between the set of interacting factors that produce or damage health and the set of interacting institutions that constitute the health care system—are not well understood. It follows, then, that many other questions central to the HSA effort—for example, the relative contributions of various factors and institutions to health care costs and the degree to which costs incurred do or do not buy health—cannot be answered with more than educated guesses either.

The designers of the program were not content with best guesses. They seem to have believed that the HSAs could either do or use scientific research that, once incorporated in the plans, would provide a basis for scientific regulation. Decisionmaking would consist of the application of demonstrated propositions to particular cases so as to yield an entirely reasoned and nonarbitrary finding. But in most cases either no general proposition exists that has been proved beyond dispute or the juxtaposition of general proposition and particular facts fails to yield a single logical, determinate solution. The plan may be made comprehensive by compiling exhaustive lists of factors, institutions, and hypothesized relationships. It may be made sophisticated by discussing the evidence for and against major hypotheses. But it cannot also be simultaneously scientific and specific in its regulatory applications. The expected smooth transition between plan as product and plan as regulatory input is anything but smooth.

Even if the intellectual demands of scientific planning were met, the

63. Cain and Darling, "Health Planning in the United States," p. 15.
64. Ibid., pp. 15–16.
65. Ibid.
66. Ibid.

institutional demands probably could not be. Planning of such scale and complexity must be broken down into special work units. This division of labor may, as illustrated above, lead to coordination problems among different persuasions within the planning organization itself. This problem, which can greatly hamper the work even of coordinating organizations with relatively clear-cut and focused goals, is of key importance to the HSAs.[67] Their mission is too broad, complex, and unfocused for easy institutionalization and can be institutionalized only at the price of a continual struggle, often abandoned or lost, for an agencywide, "comprehensive" agenda.

It is a myth that regulation must or can be based on a wide range of scientific propositions integrated in plans. Regulation inevitably involves a large measure of educated guesswork, that is, holding the regulated to standards based on best available or suggestive, but not conclusive or airtight, evidence. That regulation is inevitably arbitrary to some extent does not mean that it is also necessarily "capricious," notwithstanding the language of the Administrative Procedures Act. Steps can be taken to ensure that the guessers and the guesses are as educated as possible; that administrative procedures for exception-making and redress exist, and that the promulgators of the statutes, rules, or decisions containing the regulations have the obligation and opportunity to review them periodically in light of new evidence and of accumulating experience with their workings in the real world.[68] The negotiating forums working within these regulatory constraints also offer safeguards. This, alas, is the best a government determined to contain health care costs can do. Science will no more generate a planned solution than the market will yield an unplanned one.

"Reforms" in the Planning Program

There is wide disagreement about the proper fate of the planning program. At one extreme, the Reagan administration would end the federal

67. For a case in point see Ely Devons, "The Problem of Co-ordination in Aircraft Production," in Alec Cairncross, ed., *Papers on Planning and Economic Management by Ely Devons* (Manchester: Manchester University Press, 1970), pp. 37–58.

68. In the United States there are more abundant opportunities for influencing regulations and for exercising oversight over them than is often supposed. See Bruce C. Vladeck, "The Market vs. Regulation: The Case for Regulation," *Milbank Memorial Fund Quarterly/ Health and Society*, vol. 59 (Spring 1981), pp. 209–23. Recent far-reaching discussions about, and changes in, the regulation of the airline, trucking, and telecommunication industries suggest that once agreement has been reached on the need for regulation, "reform" may come more quickly and easily than traditional capture and iron triangle theories maintain.

role in health planning (although the states would be free to retain the HSAs and the rest with their own authority and funds if they chose) in hopes of introducing the competitive, market-based system with which planning is thought to interfere. At the other extreme some planning enthusiasts would enact regional "caps"—aggregate annual ceilings on capital and perhaps other spending for health purposes—and would give the HSAs a central role in allocating these budgets among categories.

The cap proposal has its theoretical merits but thus far little political appeal. The competition proposal has generated some political support (at least in the administration and in parts of the academic community), but its merits are questionable.[69] An essay on structural issues in the health planning program is not the place to address these very dramatic policy shifts, however, and the concluding discussion here will address itself to a middle-range question: what changes in the structure of the health planning program might improve its workings?

Unfortunately the arguments developed here suggest that structural reforms will make little difference. For example, some recommend a reduction in the role of the federal government, especially the federal bureaucracy, and would even turn the planning process over to the states in the form of health revenue sharing or block grant funds. To be sure, federal efforts to mandate rigor without offering practical advice on how to fulfill this mandate have their costs. As noted above, the emphasis on quantification and technique tends to bore and intimidate consumers, confining debate increasingly to staff, who seem to grasp the conceptual complexities, and providers, who grasp the importance of making sure that whatever the latest proposed formulas and criteria may mean, they will not mean less for providers' institutions. But these pressures also have their benefits. Those applying the pressures hold the accurate belief that many HSAs, left on their own, would write plans so general and vague that virtually nothing—no acquisition or expansion request, no proposed federal grant—would ever be "inconsistent" with them. In regulation a start must be made somewhere: standards and criteria that seem to be reasonable on the whole must be negotiated, adopted, and tried out and then retained, fine-tuned, or abandoned in the light of experience. Federal officials and HSA planners may speak of scientific rigor, but they settle in practice (as they must) for applications of conventional wisdom and common sense to local situations. Even this is accomplished only by considerable arm-twisting and consen-

69. See Lawrence D. Brown, "Competition and Health Cost Containment: Cautions and Conjectures," in ibid., pp. 145–89.

sus-forcing, and it is questionable whether HSAs are the right institutional locus for such consensus-forcing. But if the nation decides to retain HSAs with a regulatory role, then some federal consensus-forcing should be retained too.

Even if one cheerfully relieved the federal bureaucracy of all participation in the program, all the major difficulties of the HSAs would remain. Federal pressures have generally aimed to influence the *form* of local planning more than its substance; the lack of substance in many HSA plans has little to do with the federal government. The basic problems—making practical sense of an ambitious mission, managing the subunits of a complex organization, influencing related programs over which HSAs have no power, devising a proper consumer role, generating a local constituency for cost containment, drawing and applying comprehensive plans in the absence of the substantive knowledge such plans demand, and more—would all remain severe in a devolved health planning program.

A second school of structural reformers would change the role of the HSAs vis-à-vis their organizational environment—the PSROs, CON staffs, rate-setters, SHPDAs, and SHCCs. One can imagine any number of formal clearance mechanisms obliging PSROs, CON staffs, and rate-setters to take fuller account of HSAs: memorandums of understanding, coordinating liaisons and councils, review and sign-off requirements, and more come readily to mind. But these formal clearance mechanisms will probably generate paperwork and little more because of the facts of bureaucratic life: discrepancies in definitions of role, mission, and "distinctive competence"; struggles over bureaucratic turf; diverse channels of financing and grants-in-aid; and the relatively low utility of many HSA plans to date.[70] It may be expected that the views and work of the HSAs will be treated with respect by other agencies when, and only when, the HSAs are thought to address these agencies' concerns pertinently. This happy day may never come, and federal interorganizational coordination-forcing is unlikely to hasten its arrival.

Conversely, some would argue not for greater HSA leverage over state-level decisions, but for greater state influence on HSA decisions. If the basic problem is that the HSA approach "places the primary responsibility for planning at the substate regional levels" and thereby "gives precedence to local perspectives," whereas "most if not all of the problems require

70. On the limits of formal coordination in the health efforts of one state, see Basil J. F. Mott, *Anatomy of a Coordinating Council* (University of Pittsburgh Press, 1968).

statewide and national perspectives to be seen in their true dimensions,"[71] then why not strengthen statewide perspectives? A proper discussion of this question lies beyond the scope of this essay, but a quick illustration suggests that such strengthening is easier said than done. Some indication of the potential and limits of strong state leadership may be gained from recent events in Michigan. In most states the planning process is highly fragmented. In Michigan, however, influence is more easily concerted. There the major political actors, the "big three" auto companies and the United Auto Workers, have expressed much public concern about cost containment and in the late 1970s joined with Blue Cross to persuade the legislature to adopt a law calling for bed closures in the near future. This approach has been described as the most stringent assault on excess beds made to date in the United States. It is doubtful that this "interest group centralization" can be duplicated in many other states, however; the sociopolitical structure of Michigan is in these respects highly distinctive.

Adopting the plan and implementing it are two different matters, moreover. The HSA covering Detroit appointed a twenty-nine-member commission to devise a bed reduction plan in its jurisdiction. These efforts immediately evoked charges of racism from black physicians and members of the black community and other protests from osteopaths and various hospital spokesmen and staffs eager to protect their turf.[72] The state then postponed implementation of the Detroit reduction while it considered the question anew, and as of early 1981, the outcome remains in doubt. Early in 1980 a key participant summarized his evaluation of HSA planning in the atypically ambitious and rigorous context of the Michigan law: "These days I use the time driving into Detroit for the HSA meetings outlining the book I'm going to write about the health planning process: I'll call it 'Anatomy of a Failure.' "

An alternative to ambitious bed reduction legislation is the strong determination of state officials to get deeply involved in HSA planning and to hold the HSA's feet to the fire. This too is easier said than done. The same problems of regulatory equity now troubling Detroit arise wherever a state government makes a serious effort to close hospitals serving the poor, usu-

71. Mott, "The New Health Planning System," p. 245.

72. One of the more temperate accounts summarizes the issue in these terms: "Consider the 'highly technical' problem of evaluating the efficiency and effectiveness of sixty-one Detroit area hospitals in order to determine its bed reduction plan. Many of the proxy measures being used are automatically loaded in favor of the larger, tertiary care facilities, a seemingly technical decision with profound political overtones and possibly perilous consequences for access for the underserved." Consumer Coalition for Health, "Written Submission," pp. 2–3.

ally the black poor, in central city areas. New York State has been uncommonly agressive in its efforts to close down "unneeded" hospitals in New York City and it has usually enjoyed the support of the city's mayor. The community, however, has taken a different view and, aided by the local HSA, by lawsuits, by eleventh-hour federal money, and in other ways, has fought to prevent these closings.

Moreover, state activism can lead, ironically, to elaborate and possibly dysfunctional applications of the "law of anticipated reactions." For example, some observers argue that the knowledge that the state will have the final word on CON reviews encourages HSAs to avoid starting fights with local providers. If an unusually poor or unjustified project goes through, the state will raise objections—and take the heat. Yet HSA planners who may happily defer to the state then complain vociferously that the state has emasculated and mocked what was intended to be a local process when these more central actors question their work.[73]

A third category of reforms would change the present organizational structure of health planning. If, as argued here, the effort is too decentralized and participatory to work well, one might consider some structural variations that alter the organizational character of the planning agency, the level of government at which planning occurs, or both. A highly decentralized, weakly bureaucratized planning approach is not the only option. For example, planning may be decentralized but highly bureaucratized, as is much city ("master") planning. The problem here is that unless the bureaucrat planners and their products enjoy the confidence of their political superiors, their plans will gather dust on a shelf.[74] Planning may be highly centralized but relatively nonbureaucratic, as was the Office of War Mobilization and Reconversion, described by Herman Somers.[75] This presidential agency made decisions of great importance with a small, hard-working staff headed by an executive (James Byrnes) who enjoyed the highest presidential trust. But this was a wartime expedient, terminated as soon as the war ended, and no one proposes anything like it in the health care field today.

73. HSA participants sometimes complain of the other side of the coin: state CON staffs come under pressure from governors and legislators mobilized by provider interests and reverse tough HSA positions. Both patterns exist; it is now impossible to judge their relative frequency.

74. Edward C. Banfield and James Q. Wilson, *City Politics* (Harvard University Press, 1963), chap. 14.

75. Herman Somers, *Presidential Agency: The Office of War Mobilization and Reconversion* (Harvard University Press, 1950).

There are highly centralized and highly bureaucratic arrangements such as the wage and price control bodies established in the Nixon administration.[76] The problems encountered by bodies of this kind—bureaucratic inflexibility or seeming arbitrariness in the face of an endless parade of requests for exceptions to general rules—are essentially the opposite of those encountered in the HSAs, which struggle with an inability to formulate general rules and a cheerful willingness to concede exceptions to the rules that are devised.

These alternatives offer little more than mental exercise, although this exercise recalls a simple but important point: the decision to avoid larger measures of centralization and bureaucracy in health planning at once reflects important social values and entails certain social costs. The HSA approach offers the satisfaction of responsiveness—"doing something"— at the price of effectiveness, that is, substantive accomplishment.[77] In health care as in other fields, the confident term "planning" conceals a multitude of hesitations and confusions.

Finally, a modest structural change worth considering is that of introducing a more rational division of labor in the HSAs by changing the sequence of interaction of the participants and the roles they play. The current practice essentially entrusts all tasks to all participants; activities are divided up largely as the participants choose but in ways that preserve a round table mix of consumer and provider interests at each stage. One might consider matching tasks to the strengths of the participants, however. For example, one might borrow a principle from the theory of legislative-executive relations: the more expert branch (the executive, at the head of the bureaucracy) should initiate proposals and do the detail-work; the less specialized, more commonsensical, more directly accountable branch (the legislative) should review (oversee) and amend these proposals from the layman's viewpoint. Applying this principle to the planning process, it could be argued that providers, who have expertise, professional legitimacy, detailed institutional knowledge, and intensity of preferences on their side, should initiate first drafts of local health plans. Then, consumers and representatives of special groups might review the drafts, press questions, hear the appeals of disaffected providers, and negotiate over additions, deletions, and changes. It might be a good thing to endow the consumer side with a sizable professional staff of its own. (This, for example,

76. Robert Kagin, *Regulatory Justice* (New York: Russell Sage Foundation, 1978).
77. Lawrence D. Brown, "The Formulation of Federal Health Care Policy," *Bulletin of the New York Academy of Medicine*, vol. 54 (January 1978), pp. 45–58, especially pp. 56–58.

was an early and insistent demand of citizen participants in the model cities program. The neighborhood representatives were convinced, probably correctly, that without a staff of their own they could not hope to keep pace with municipal agencies.) State government could stand by as an arbitrator, with authority to devise a plan of its own if the locals failed to reach agreement within a reasonable time. Both state and federal approval of the plans would be required, giving these governments some bargaining leverage too. This approach offers a more reasonable division of labor than the present mingling of skills at every stage. It arrives at decisions by a structured sequence of planning, review, negotiation, amendment, and approval, not by round table discussions that leave the final word to large, part-time, and often uncohesive boards and SHCCs.

Structural changes might improve the planning process at the margin, but no one should expect them to affect fundamentally the problems from which HSAs now suffer. Their basic problems lie not in their structures but rather in the breadth, heterogeneity, and complexity of their mission. As long as the HSAs are asked simultaneously to be research, planning, regulatory, and advocacy bodies, their way will not be smooth. As long as they are asked to assume these four roles *and* to make a "demonstrable difference" in costs, in the delivery system, in health status, in access (and so on and on), they will be bound to disappoint.

Then why not change their missions? In particular, why not distinguish the academic functions of research, planning, and perhaps advocacy from regulation and relieve the HSAs of responsibility for the latter? Almost everyone agrees that the HSAs need time to pull themselves together and show results. But the regulatory component of the mission robs them of time by insistently flinging down the gauntlet of "demonstrable differences." HSAs could instead be treated as merit goods, as community debating, deliberating, and consensus-building associations, as not-all-that expensive luxuries that an indulgent society can easily afford.

Furthermore, it is doubtful that even endless grants of time and money will turn the HSAs into effective regulators. Regulation, it was argued above, demands not consumer-dominated pluralism but exertions of political will; not self-regulating localism but a strong measure of detachment from the local milieu, that is, a greater measure of centralization at the federal (or perhaps at the state) level; not scientifically grounded planning but rather a determination to translate best reasonable guesses into laws and regulations and then remain sensitive to the need for change. On each count, the presuppositions of the HSAs place regulation on precisely the wrong footing. If the HSAs need relief from regulation, regulation equally needs relief from the HSAs.

But something might be lost after all from such relief. Although no sensible observer would contend that the HSAs have much improved people's health, dramatically increased access to care, or (still less) saved the system much money, they do appear to be making three less flamboyant contributions, at least in some places. First, they have exerted themselves on behalf of neglected areas and "priorities" of medical service, such as mental health, prevention, ambulatory care, and so on, that find few strong institutional advocates among local organizations. Second, they have put pressure on local institutions, especially hospitals, to devote more resources, attention, and sympathy to the needs of the poor. And third, they are a useful counterbalance to various elites contending for dominance over health care policy.

This third point deserves brief amplification. Governmental elites at all three levels of government are mainly concerned with saving money albeit without "too much" regulation or other causes of aggravation. Analytic elites, based mainly in the academic community, clamor for the chance to apply in public policy their latest syllogism purporting to demonstrate that (by means of market approaches, competition, incentives, or whatever) much money can be saved with no threat to access, to quality, or to other legitimate ends. Provider elites argue for their professional autonomy and for high levels of remuneration. Consumer elites in proliferating consumer protection organizations claim a unique legitimacy in representing the voice of the average man and woman in health policy questions.

These elites respond to budgetary, intellectual, professional, and organizational incentives and maintenance needs, respectively. They are liable to be swept up in their particular perspectives and interests and to lose touch with popular opinion. The HSA process reminds these elites that out there amid the common folk there is still more interest in access than in efficiency, in preserving and equalizing than in cost cutting. This contribution has little to do with cost containment, but the HSAs' ability to make it probably depends importantly on preserving the limited regulatory leverage they now enjoy. Without a formal voice in grant reviews, their views on local medical priorities might not be heard. Without the power to delay and bargain over CON applications, they might be unable to pressure local hospitals into doing more for the poor. Without the presumption that the local plan stands for and is to be used for something, contending elites might find it convenient to ignore local sentiment.

There is irony, of course, in the observation that agencies endowed with regulatory powers in hopes that they would use them to strike a blow for cost containment are using them partly to contain the cost containers,[78] and there is double irony in the contention that they may need to retain regulatory powers precisely to enable them to go on striking blows that probably raise health care costs. Perhaps then the proper policy response is finally to throw irony over in favor of logic. After all, there are better, more equitable ways of honoring neglected priorities and groups than by means of local organizational pressure: by committing new federal money to support these priorities and by extending, refining, and enforcing the legal entitlements of medicaid recipients, for example. And although there may be nothing like a grass roots organization to express grass roots sentiment, this is not the last word in representation. A pluralistic, federal system like that in the United States has *layers* of representation, and it is far from obvious which layer or mix of layers is most suitable to represent public opinion on a given policy question.[79] Who is to say that local concern about keeping underused maternity wards alive and well should be treated as a more authoritative, representative datum than the concern of a U.S. president or congressional committee with the frightening growth of health care expenditures over time? One need not pose policy questions so as to elicit highly detailed local preferences, and sometimes one should not.

78. For instance, the head of New York City's HSA describes his agency as a means of providing alternatives to the efforts of public officials to "take drastic measures to shrink the health care system." The HSA, he believes, is "uniquely suited" to this task because its "orientation toward health and health planning enables us to avoid the danger of overemphasizing cost savings for their own sake." His HSA has taken "the bold and ambitious step of undertaking a series of related studies. . . ." Anthony L. Watson, "The View From the Health System Agency," *Bulletin of the New York Academy of Medicine*, vol. 56 (January-February 1980), pp. 56, 57.

79. In the United States the layers might be described as follows: (1) communitarian—decisions made in open, round table, town meeting forums; (2) participatory—decisions made by a self-selected subset of activist community residents; (3) pluralist—decisions made by the interaction of local groups and organizations along with either of the two modes above; (4) corporatist—decisions made by organizations deliberately selected to represent major sectoral interests (along with any of the three modes above); (5) political-legal—decisions made by a subset of community residents formally chosen by election (along with the four modes above); (6) bureaucratic—decisions made by officials appointed by and accountable to political representatives; and (7) federal—decisions made by the interaction of some or all of the processes above between higher and lower levels of government. Decisionmaking might involve one, some, or all of these layers. Each has its distinctive strengths and weaknesses. The "optimal" representative layer or mix of layers for policymaking in a democracy is therefore a more complex question than much loose political theorizing about "participation" would suggest.